cluster

ALSO BY SOUVANKHAM THAMMAVONGSA

Small Arguments (2003)
Found (2007)
Light (2013)

cluster

POEMS BY

SOUVANKHAM THAMMAVONGSA

McClelland & Stewart

McClelland & Stewart and colophon are registered trademarks of
Penguin Random House Canada Limited.

The authorized representative in the EU for product safety and compliance is
Penguin Random House Ireland, Morrison Chambers, 32 Nassau Street,
Dublin D02 YH68, Ireland. https://eu-contact.penguin.ie

Library and Archives Canada Cataloguing in Publication

Thammavongsa, Souvankham, 1978-, author
Cluster / Souvankham Thammavongsa.

Poems.

ISBN 978-0-7710-7098-3 (softcover)

I. Title.

PS8589.H3457C58 2019   C811'.6   C2018-903253-7

Published simultaneously in the United States of America by
McClelland & Stewart, a division of Penguin Random House Canada Limited.

ISBN: 978-0-7710-7098-3
ebook ISBN: 978-0-7710-7099-0

Typeset in Requiem by M&S, Toronto
Printed in the United States of America

McClelland & Stewart
a division of Penguin Random House Canada Limited
320 Front Street West, Suite 1400
Toronto, Ontario, M5V 3B6, Canada
penguinrandomhouse.ca

Penguin
Random House
McCLELLAND & STEWART

Contents

cluster

CLUSTER

The story they told us was wide and lost and ever changing

And the words it came with were small

Sprawling and crawling for its end

The end, if something could be said of it

Tried to take shadow and shape but closed and collapsed at its centre

Wound around an end a different coloured string

There might have been an umbrella, shoe, or even jewellery

But who among us would know our way back, could climb over that mess again?

Cut a hole into this page and hold it up to the sky

Tell us if it is day and the stars that kick in if it is night

Fluff the clouds if they look flat or trim the moon if it is full

Tell yourself yesterday was not tomorrow and none of it will ever be today

POSTCARD FROM THE OUTSKIRTS

Blueberries knot from the ground

Blue lustre as cold as steeled shells

Scattered and dropped throughout

A method of an organized pattern

Designed to be noticed from above

They insist they are natural this way

Nature is ruthless and very efficient

It is a prevailing wisdom no doubt

What joy then to reach in and pluck one

Your face still intact and recognizable

This act could conclude the length of life

The decision is not an individual one

But we know from what we are told

There is nothing to see here, folks

MOTHER

My mother had given birth a few months ago. I thought it

was odd, as she just turned sixty recently. I had not seen

her pregnant. But there it was in the room, all formed. A

baby boy. I didn't know what his name was, only that she told

me I could have him, if I wanted, she didn't really care. And

I told her I didn't want him. And when I did, she picked him

up, and as she did this, I noticed at the back of his head, a third

grey eye. It had opened and blinked and then closed. She took

him to another room down the hall and I followed. Then, she

stumbled and fell, collapsed. I ran to her, to pick her up. Her whole

face was gone, peeled back, and her eyes weren't even there. I

picked her up like she was my own child and held her. I was sorry

I wasn't there sooner. And all this time, I did not think of that child.

The one with the third grey eye. I only thought of her now,

who she had been to me then, and if she would be that again.

We used to have this poster on the wall. It was
an advertisement for Minute Maid. A row of
orange groves. It went on top of billboards
and was sealed inside the glass of bus shelters.
The poster gave my parents a different view
than the one we had from our window. We
had only snow and the exhaust pipe from a car
parked just outside. The poster never tore.
A kind of paper built for the weather here.
From far away, the blue in the sky and the green
on the ground looked uniform. Up close
they were made of a million little dots. The blue
was made of blue, but the green was of bits
of blue and yellow arranged on top of each other.
The yellow came first and then the blue. It was
the distant looking that brought them together,
that filled the space between them. This poster
was our future looking in on us, but we didn't see.
We didn't see how inside it would be my mother
picking oranges in that field. Her nails cut short
but dirt still found its way there. And her hair
would feel like straw and half her face would sag from
a stroke. She says not to think on it too much,
she can't taste anything on one side except bitterness.

What had once been many shades of sun

and cloud and what we had predicted to have

a chance of is now. The face looking at us is

an outline floating in with two eyes and

a mouth. This face could be ours looking back

from some past we're going toward or just an

expression trying to keep us out. Whatever it is

does not matter. Wanting to live does. If

it is saying something we can't stop for it. If it is

reporting the future and says what's happened

sew it shut and anchor it to sink and to stay sunk.

We were going before anyone could call us gone.

PREGNANT

In Lao, it is *teu phaa*

It means to hold a split, to hold a splitting, to carry around a split

Whatever you think you are or was, split

Not split open and broken away, but the split that is still hinged there, the coming-apart that hadn't caught on to anything to break off

To have never carried that split, to not know

What then do you know you have:

A sanding-down, a knowledge of repair and mechanic, how to keep wood to wood

WE ALWAYS LIVED WITH MICE

My mother grabbed at them with her bare hands

Their heads looked the other way when she broke them

When I removed them from the traps I would stare

And try to remember each of their refined features

I checked the genitals, the shape of claws, the shade of fur

The one I remember the most didn't die right away

It had a different shape, heavy in the middle, swollen teats

I thought of this one and what I did

All the ants ate poison from the tin in the corner of the bathroom walls

How the label said they would crawl back to the colony and explode

An announcement is coming this afternoon.

Something about targeted closings, forecasts,

assuming of sales, royalty revenues, gross proceeds,

multiple metrics, range of approximation, land

holdings, future spending, and commitments.

Watch how rank can be stronger than peers. More

details will be provided at the closing of this transaction.

Defer any major decisions. Resume spending and

expansion. Deploy capital to improve physical

integration. Main concerns are related to potential use

of proceeds. Return to historical capital, ongoing

internal changes. There is an implied discount.

Proceeds and recommendation remain unchanged.

Continue to rank. Repeat. Buy. Press release.

BROKERAGE REPORT II

It's robust. The complex dynamics
of a particular cycle. Prices can
move higher. Oil wells naturally
decline. Drill new wells. Concerns
have been raised. Released already
today. Proves to be correct. Robust.
In the long run. The pace is slower
than some investors would like.
Nevertheless a trend is encouraging.
The rest of the world. It's robust.
Notwithstanding concerns. We do not
recommend aggressive weighting
at this time. In summary, given
the difficulty of predicting and time,
we do remain optimistic. A leader in
this space. The universe remains
the same. Robust. It's robust.
Trends. The risks could be amplified.

SUMMER

Everything
is dying.
The assortment
of flowers
drooped to
their hanging.
The cherry tree
had no fruit
this year. The
walnuts fall
on our roof
every two minutes,
relentless,
without mercy.
The bees
don't come
around. Our
neighbour
bought an urn
yesterday.
His wife
is off life
support. The
funeral has
been arranged.

WINTER

Everything
is alive
and in its
full bloom.
The daffodils
hold
their heads
high,
signalling
their value.
The snow
is gone. Bird
nests
made visible
by their
chirping.
The sun,
its horrible
hot light
unbearably
everywhere.

LAST DAY AT THE OFFICE

It was the potted plants that were
the first to go. Someone had been assigned
the task of watering them, and whoever

that was didn't come around to do it,
and if there had been a replacement
it wasn't listed as part of the job.

Then, it was the pens in the office
and the envelopes and metal-ringed notepads.
Someone was put in charge of buying

the supplies and stocking the drawer.
There are paperclips and staples at
least. Next, it was the window. You

could see across an alleyway to the side
of a Hilton Hotel. When it rained, the cement
got darker. And when the desks

were all moved to the fourth floor, where
there was no window at all, we were glad
for a door on a broken hinge. We

opened the door to keep our spirits up. The
cheques they gave us didn't clear.
A stamp with "Insufficient funds" angled

across the amount it was made out for.
Finally, the last day there arrived. It was
obvious. There was a man sitting in

the lunchroom, belching. He didn't bother
to apologize or excuse himself as if
all these years made us family now. In the

washroom stall, the ceiling was about to collapse.
There was a brown stain there, growing wide.
A broken pipe, a busted toilet. Someone

hadn't seen to it by now. There had been
a custodian. He wore a grey uniform and smoked
near the front entrance during his breaks. He

was there when a woman got run over.
He took off his jacket and folded it neatly
under the woman's head. He kneeled down

beside her to get her last word. Something
was said, but what that was between the two
of them I couldn't know. We were all removed.

A SEAHORSE

moves

        at its own dumb pace,

                dancing

        quietly

                    underneath

          the ocean's current, spinning

unalarmed

        by what's happening

     or what's happened

By all accounts,

there is

no record

for its rank

above

MY MOTHER GAVE ME

a photo album. There were a handful

of pictures and I am the same age

in every one. There is one photo of me

and my father on the day he taught me

how to ride my bike. We are laughing

and in the lower left corner is a small

boy sitting on a park bench watching us.

He's my brother. I always thought

he was the favourite one, the one

they really wanted. I did not think

of what I might have looked like to him.

He is looking on in this photo, sitting

on a park bench. He does not have a bike

of his own. It is the same with his clothes.

The clothes he wore had been mine,

green overalls, blue shirt, all the winter jackets

and snowsuits. Never knowing the feel of new

things. Even the haircut he has is mine.

In a few years, he too will have this bike.

But no one will have taken the time to teach

him how to ride it without the training wheels

because they had come off years before. He

will ride this bike as I left it, like everything else

I had, and it will still be pink and the flowers printed

will still be there. There will be no picture of that day.

There is only a picture of this day.

This day of him sitting on the park bench alone,

hands in his lap, looking on and waiting for his turn.

GAYATRI

I have a picture of us when we are seven
but we aren't in it. At the time it was taken

we thought we were. We posed with our wide
grins and best-friends-forever certainty. I angled

the camera to capture us in front of a Christmas tree.
All the sparkling tinsel and dangling silver balls aren't there.

There is only the ceiling and the tip
of the pine needle. There isn't a star or an angel

on top. I have kept this picture of us for years,
the only one to remember and laugh at what happened

to us then. It was taken before a time you could
see a picture on a screen, see how it turned out

and decide whether it was worth keeping. I think of you
now and again, the plain peanut butter sandwiches we ate

with apples. You said you were going to be a dentist
when you grow up, and with a fork and a spoon

you determined it was possible I would live
and sent me home with a bag full of Twizzlers and hair bands.

ZEVART

Every day at lunchtime, you gave me half
your sandwich. I never went hungry because

of you. I remember your cowboy boots, the ones
you liked in grade eleven, the time we sat together

on the stage at the last dance
waiting for someone to ask us. We walked

home together every day for thirteen years, saved
our pennies and tallied up enough

to buy a Hot Lip candy we could split. You know,
I still have the letters you wrote to me, the ones

you'd fold over six times to form a small pyramid.
They all seem to say the same thing inside about love,

how it can't be hurried, how there can only be one,
and today could be the day that changes everything.

BROKERAGE REPORT III

Yield. Energy prices sank

today. Focus on rising

earnings instead. Bigger

profits and a higher finish.

Minimize costs, be efficient.

Turbines and plastics,

steel and rubber, scrap metal.

Oil futures fell sharply.

The standard. Adjust profits,

move margins, beat

projections. Investors are

concerned, analysts expect.

The index gave up and closed.

Yield. Bond prices can turn.

Tariff wars, but copper remains.

BROKERAGE REPORT IV

After disclosures, figures
are up. A year ago
trends revealed
flattened growth. This
morning we reported.
Our recommendation
is to hold. The dive in price
plunges below expectation.
We cannot expand. There
are limits. Raise questions.
Compound bad news. Veiled
numbers at this point
remain veiled. Net loss
should narrow property.
This shift should emphasize
appeal. Blame workers
and redesign the universe.
Curate material, side-step
the issue. Caution growth.
Continue and remain within
margins. Standard and poor.

NINE O'CLOCK

It is nine o'clock

and it has been

nine o'clock all day

The battery gone

unplugged perhaps

the metal plates

turning underneath

stopped the tick-tock

It would be unwise

to say it's incorrect

because it is nine

o'clock somewhere

or for someone it'll

become nine o'clock

or nine o'clock will

get to be for someone. It's

the start of the working

day where time is money

and money is time or

the end of the day if

the day was for working

or counting up that way

What time it really is

I don't know and can't tell

It could very well be

nine o'clock but I can't say

with much certainty or

confidence in that matter

If I were to look outside

for the shade and shadow

around where I stood

I wouldn't see it on the ground

in front of me. And from

where I stood and was standing

I couldn't look behind

or bring myself to turn

WHALES

I can spot the whales

They come up for air

A sprout in the ocean

I tell everyone to look

But by the time they turn

The whales have gone back

I have spotted about five

Now, they don't even have

To show themselves

I know they are there

The seagulls circle them

Waiting for what they didn't kill

LANDING

When flying make

allowances for

the direction of wind

Know the speed

and direction of

a plane in still air

Know where the wind

will push off, know

the course you set

for yourself

Compensate and fly

in the direction

of the vector,

refer to diagrams

and express each sum,

aim always to land

MANUAL FOR DIVING

The centre of gravity on a diving body

Is somewhere in the middle of the gut

This is a point that is fixed

The arms rotate, the legs stay together, toes point

Once you enter the water whatever you do then

Doesn't count, won't be marked, won't be for the judge

There are no points for what your body didn't do

Or for what your body could do in the routine

All the points are for what you do on the springboard

And the space your leap takes up

Points for how you lean, how you rotate and spin, and when

Even how you enter the water and the splash you make

There are no points once you're under

What you do there won't cost you a thing

ANTS

I had
been

thinking
of

my own
funeral

and what
that

would
look like

I want
it

to be
like this

Someone
would

take
notice

and turn,
order

the others
to get

in
the line

and take
me

from where
I'd been

And all
would

pass
the body

back
down

one by one
by one

until I reached
the last

There,
I'd be

lowered
into soil

and I
would

fill
the hole

I didn't
make

Workers at the mine are on strike.
There is gold at the site. Machines
were delivered last quarter. It was
all set to rise. This delay should
not worry investors. New workers
are being brought in. There are
proposed purchases and plans,
collapsed acquisitions, but we remain
positive and project. Gold is not
an upstart in this decade. A new
empire will not rise and become
a digital asset in this field. There
is nothing digital about gold. We
cannot emphasize rocks and form.
We will continue and oversee,
operate and focus, and take aim.
The stakes are high. It had long
been anticipated for closure, but
we will not dismantle our deal.
Our profits remain at the site.

PICTURE OF US

in Florida, at Busch Gardens.
I am twelve, standing in tall

grass by a roller coaster. I am
wearing a T-Shirt, the word EARTH

printed at its centre.
The letters are so big

there isn't room for anything
else. Underneath are my

shorts, yellow circles
splattered across the front.

This is the outfit I wear all summer.
It's what I wear when we walk out

into the ocean floor at low-tide
looking for a conch.

The bigger, more beautiful ones
are farther out. I won't notice

how far I've gone. By the time
I find one the tide had come back in.

A shark's grey tail circles me. I
know it is the blood between my legs.

I am not alone. A pod of dolphins come,
circling and signalling on some

ancient frequency. I get to shore,
conch shell in hand, and hold it to my ear.

Ear on ear
I hear only my own breathing.

MY MOTHER'S HOUSE

I dreamt of you this early morning

You were living in squalour

The bed you slept on wasn't made

Someone had left a puddle in it

This room you lived in was small

No windows or fixtures on the ceiling

You had not wanted me to see you like this

And took me into another room

This one had high ceilings and hardwood floors

There was a painting on the wall

It wasn't yours

All the things you made weren't there

I did not ask if you were happy

I knew you were not, not even close

You told me you were sorry

You always do

You live here now

I wasn't surprised, and, in fact, it made sense

In this small room

In a house my mother made for you in my dreams

NANDU

That year there was
a rhinoceros born
at the zoo. He weighed
140 pounds. They say
he gains five pounds
per day. He was named
Nandu, which means
one who is cheerful
and happy. I like
the name. It suits him.
I went to visit him
and signed up for
a membership card.
I was worried it was too
cold and he'd be indoors,
but there he was,
in the open. He looked
right at me and trotted
over. He lifted his head
and I could look at his face.
Then, he turned from me
and went back to his life
and let out gas. It was
putrid, natural, I guess.
Like a mother, I said,
Let it out, let it all out.
I told my mother
what happened. She
laughed and said,
"No one wants to be
a mother. You don't know
until you are."

A PEBBLE

has

   so much

      to say

           You

      threw it

      out

          across water,

             thinking

                 it couldn't

     do anything there,

but it lifted

itself up

and took

down

a gulp

you couldn't

keep sunk

O

When this letter is written out by hand

Where it begins and ends land in the same place

It is a gesture to single out what isn't perfect

It marks an outside and an inside

And you get to decide where that is

It means what it says

It's so matter-of-fact

Upper case or lower case it still looks the same

Sometimes it's a number signifying nothing

Until it's an investment return

Any other figure followed by 0 pushes its value higher

It is a mark of temperature

A degree to balance the consequence of liquid states

Everything in the universe has this shape

You don't have to see it for yourself for it to be true

This letter is the shape of a tennis ball

At Wimbledon during play the tennis ball always bounces

It gets caught up in the net or hits the side of a racket

There's always a count to keep

In Laos, a child wanted to play with a ball

He found one buried in the ground

It did not bounce

He took it home to his family

Everyone turned out inside

The thing did what it didn't do before

It bounced

Nothing happens if you're lucky

Foraging for dinner

Harvesting the next cycle of crops

Walking or digging

Disturbing ground

This is how you lose an arm or leg

All of it

You can't eat metal

But this is the new cash crop

More than forty years ago, it had been planted

Designed and seeded to clear the trail

"There are no American combat forces in Laos"

You don't have to declare a war for there to be one

You could say it never happened

Who would know

We move through fragments every day and we live

A fragment isn't the whole of a thing

But it doesn't need to be

It's enough to be an open

An open that opens something inside and never closes itself up again

This summer a dam collapsed in Laos

The area of detail is marked with a little o

Missing is the view of a human face on that map

Over 6,600 were displaced and hundreds more were still missing

A company dispatched rescue and emergency relief

One helicopter and 11 boats

It was a billion-dollar project

They were worried about personnel

A few ambulances streaked by

We are told an investigation is underway

A dam collapsed

We already know about the failure of structure

But they want to study it now

They want to study dam standards and dam safety

While people scramble to higher ground

Wait on rooftops and trees stranded on slopes

The weather, we are told, is an obstacle

And authorities are looking for mattresses

There is an effort to rescue

Repeated phone calls go unanswered

An expert on Laos from the University of Wisconsin

Was brought in to comment

His word was quoted by *The New York Times*

The experts on Laos

Are those who live there

In the house abandoned and turned on its side

On the oxen half-hidden in knee-deep water

There was no warning, they said

Just someone calling "The water is coming"

The water is coming

It was there

Every eight minutes, 24 hours a day, 260 million rained down

80 million failed to explode

The war is over we are told

Troops have been sent home

The groundwork remains

Proving there is no such thing as time

It doesn't respect or forgive or lessen anything

A decision was made a long time ago

The carrying-out crops up

And you move it to the side of the field or plant around it

Fashion it into a metal necklace

Use as stilts for homes or a table lamp

"Best Detroit steel" is the uptick trend

One man tossed it into a basket on his back

The ball-bearings it threw out went through his chest

An aim and target chosen years ago

The still-centre of a spin

The smallest unit of ordinary matter

Indivisible until it is

Meaning

It can happen with so little

It can take a long time to arrive

Years even if ever

It's possible meaning doesn't mean anything

And that is its meaning

Meaning doesn't give you clarity

Clarity isn't meaning

Clutter and garbage can have meaning

The cleaning-up that needed to be done

Left for someone else to take care of

Someone who has nothing to do with its meaning

But will do the work to mean

Whatever happens to meaning

It is always there

Orbiting a set path

Attached and revolving

A quiet hum behind a wall

It means something even if you don't want it

And when you want it

It doesn't matter how voluminous

It doesn't mean at all

THERE ARE NO PHOTOGRAPHS OF ME

In all the photographs
you took

I'm
not there

I managed
to get out

before
the flash

Sometimes
there was my foot

or splash
of black hair

You'd point
to that

and say
it was me

that
I had been there

but who could say
that's true

I am looking
at the photographs

you have
now

I'm not there
and

I haven't been there
for years

I can see
the frame

of the
photograph

I can see further
than that

I can see
outside

this frame
the looking on

NORTH

It's the direction a compass is always pointing

The part of a map that shows a view of the world

It's still there pointing when you're upside down

Wind speed is a fundamental atmospheric quantity

Changes in temperature are a determining factor

Look for the sun and track where it rises and sets

Tell from the shape your shadow casts for you

It will matter to know where you are and when

You might need all these days or hours to count

You will never be more alone following this point

Some place you haven't been yet rotating past

Wherever you are you aren't there even when you *are*

A SPIDER

made

    this

It hadn't been

    damaged

and if it had been,

    it was built back

        over night

Over and over

    from some small

        dark pit,

it spun out

a whole world

for itself

Nothing

could come close

and even in its brevity

it will outlast

our dim little buildings

I saw a dead man by the side of the road. I stopped

To look at him. I had never seen one up close like this.

He did not look dead. There was no blood, no scene

Of accident. Maybe he fell from somewhere, run over

By a passing car. I wanted to touch him, to feel what

Being dead felt like, but I did not. There was no one

Around to see him, to call to gather for him. Nothing

But my own feeling. I spoke like I had been loved

For many years, like he had been mine. And then, I

Went on, walked around the body, left the burying.

I would see one just like him out on the lake again.

Alone and swimming. A head bobbing to the surface.

GLITTER

You
can cover

it all
up

in
this stuff

if
you want

We both
know

what's
beneath

that
glitter

None
of this

was
ever gold

or could
ever be

Little
plastic flecks

shining
only

in close
proximity

To get by
you'll

have to
agree

not
to see

what you
have

and you
agree

until
there's gold

Face
to face

you admit
you can't

make
anything

come
close to that

It was
there

before you
and

what
it took

to get
gold

like that
well, let me tell

you
don't have

to make
it do

a thing
at all

to shine

COST

The squirrel
is dead

Its eye
sockets

have been
filled in

with green
glass beads,

Four little paws
frozen

in pose, and
a fluffed-up tail

Next to other
stuffed animals

arranged in bright
cartoon colours,

fabric pocked
with balls of lint,

plastic mouths
glued open,

laughing,
all in

on some joke
they've told

The squirrel
isn't laughing,

a cost
of the matter

of having been
real once

ART

Across
the street
from the
museum
there is
someone
making
bubbles.
He has an
old mop
with two
dirt-filled
strings.
He holds
the mop
high, waves
it above
his head,
cleaning.
A bubble
the size
of a human
body
blisters
and grieves
out of air.
None of us
can climb
inside
and be
carried off.
All of us

watch
each one
float away.
He must
have made
thousands
that day,
but there is
no proof
of any
having been
made
except those
of us who
saw it,
the foam on
the ground,
dishwashing
liquid
dripping from
high-pitched
trees.

A PLASTIC BEAR

tried
to eat me

the other
night

Its jaw
came

apart,
a sad

attempt
at a loud

roar
was made

I suppose
I should

be scared
but

I reached out
to it,

to feel
up

the dark
there

It occurred
to me

the thing
didn't

have
a body

I knew then
it couldn't stomach

or keep
the spine

I splintered
to be here

BLOWFISH

My parents took us to Florida.

St. Petersburg, Florida.

We drove there in our blue Toyota van.

1990 was a good year for us but we didn't know then.

There's a photograph of all of us inside King Kong's fist.

I am in the middle.

We were supposed to pretend we were all dying but I am at the centre as
still as ever.

My mom is smiling the way you do when someone takes your picture. She
was not someone who pretended anything.

My father leans out all dramatic.

My brother mid-scream, ready as ever to be part of the show and have his
close-up.

My father made signs and my mother worked with him.

In St. Petersburg, Florida, was my uncle. He was my father's older
brother, the first-born.

My uncle took us fishing in Key West.

We dragged a net and caught shrimp, a baby shark, and a blowfish the size
  of a human eyeball. The blowfish we kept.

Because it was scared, it blew itself up, a hard round ball.

My mother loved this creature and tried to preserve it as it was dying.

She tied string around the tail, made a knot, and hung it in the backyard.

But the humidity in Florida kept it moist.

It rotted.

It started to smell, and the shape it was started to flatten and then dry out.

We drove home, back to Toronto with this blowfish rotting in the car.

The smell got to be so bad my mother put a few drops of Chanel No. 5
   perfume on it every four hours.

By the time we got home, the blowfish had shrunk to the size of a raisin.

It was only we who knew that stinking raisin had once been a blowfish.

A blowfish.

Once round, a prickly thing, full of air.

To this day, I can't stand Chanel No. 5.

It reminds me of that blowfish.

Rot. Raw.

How the thing lost its shape in the world and became a small hardness.

It's strange, isn't it?

How this rot reminds me of a time when my family was happy.

How thrilled and alive we all were together, inside King Kong's palm, his
open mouth.

We lost the shape of who we were.

And there's nothing left but that shape in the car.

The one no one else could say was alive, but us.

CHRISTMAS

We are five levels below the ground
I didn't know basements go this far down

What everyone
Is doing here is counting cash

Bags and bags and bags
Brought in by a security truck

We count this cash
Make sure it all adds up

Enter the correct amount
Right down to the penny

The cash passing through
Is not mine

I have never seen
This kind of money before

Where it comes from
Is labelled

It's all from grocery stores
Food in every brightly lit aisle

At four in the morning
We stop, form a circle, and exercise

Someone turns on music
And we move along

I didn't bring anything to eat
Didn't have time to make lunch

And a woman there knows this
She is or has been a mother before

She tells me I should eat this
This thing she made at home

It's warm
She can't possibly finish it

All by herself, she tells me
And I have some

I haven't told her anything
Not even my name

Where I've been or why
I'm here

I didn't say
What happened

What I lost
Or what's wrong

That's something people do
Up there

TWINS

I remember the evening we saw
this movie. I was eleven. My parents

just bought a van. They wanted to go
to the drive-in and we waited for it to

get dark outside. We brought along
pillows and a blanket, hot chocolate. I fell

asleep in the backseat, tired of waiting. I might
have woken up a few times because I do

remember this scene of them dancing
in a bar. I remember my parents laughing

at how these two could be twins. One giant
and the other out of shape and short. That

these two could come from the same place
at the same time and could manage all

these years apart. When I think about it,
the two of them were like that too even if

they didn't think of it like that then. I
now wish I hadn't fallen asleep that day.

I wish I had stayed awake, remembered all
the times they laughed so hard like this together.

There were so many of them. We always
had an abacus around. Maybe if I learned

how to use one, I could have shifted a few beads
and then tell you how much a lifetime costs.

THEORY OF WRITING

We all know two plus two equals four
And we begin with that. We learn to add
Before we learn how to take away, to lose.
It's a great way to learn how to write. To
Have a formula, a line to follow. Before
We know what adding means, we have to
Know what two means. What two and two
Means together. There are many ways to get to
Four. Five subtract one is equal to four.
One times four is equal to four. The square
Root of sixteen is four. A square root
Is a number that looks exactly like it, multiplied
By itself. Four divided by one also equals
Four. Four to the power of one is equal to four, too.
We can get there through a derivative, if
That's how you want it. The square of the
Hypotenuse is equal to the sum of the squares
Of the other two sides can also get you to four.
There are so many ways to get to four.
Once all these other ways of getting
To four are understood, it's not really four
You're after. Anyone can get to four. And
You know this. Maybe it's the certainty of
Four. That you can always get to it. That it will
Always turn out the same. Maybe that's what
You want. The certainty of four. Or maybe
It's the ways in which you know how
To get to four that is the point of writing. What
You had to learn and build, the time it took
To hold open that possibility for yourself.

ANOTHER PICTURE OF US

Maybe it was me who had taken this picture. My parents
are looking at the camera, unsmiling, serious, my father's

arm over my mother's shoulder. I know this picture is taken
at their friend's house. Behind them are photographs of other

people. It's cold. They are wearing sweaters. My mother's
shoes match her red leather belt and lips. They are kitten heels.

The photo isn't very clear. Dark. Maybe the flash had been
turned off. This photo had been tucked in behind another one.

It was one still intact of the two of them. I am trying to take
what I know now and try to see if I can find it here. Had it

happened here on this day or did it come apart years after.
They are the same height, all dressed up, somewhere to go.

A party, a wedding. Maybe there will be some dancing.
I hope where they are going, they will have fun and remember

all of it. I hope they remember how they were together and who
they were with. I hope they remember their love, the comfort of it,

the way it feels to know you have it. I can't see them together
like this anymore. But here we are, together, for once.

A SNAKE

thinks

    itself

        so free

shedding

    its skin

      leaving

           everything

    it was

      behind,

but when it dies

    all that's left

are the bones

      it was locked up in

They form

and bar

all the facts

inside

MANGOSTEENS

My mother taught me to pick
one. They look all the same
from the outside. You can't
tell by knocking, shaking, or
looking at the skin which
is ripe. The ones my mother
picked out, the fruit was full
and bounteous, sweet, barely
any seed. The ones I chose
opened to seeds, bitter and
furious things. She told me
to turn one upside down
and count the bumps. I picked
them like she did, brought them
to a fence I climbed over, and
gave them to you. You did
not want these things. Said
you couldn't eat anything
like that. I didn't understand.
It didn't make sense. But then,
I saw you change. Sometimes
it happened over a few days,
other times in an afternoon,
or just under an hour. It always
started with your teeth. They
chattered and chopped, then you
bit your lip and ate your mouth
and head, and you turned
to get the rest of you. Each time,
I built you back from memory,
put things in the wrong place,
further and further from what

you were. Each time, you got angry,
ranted and raved, told me this is not
the way you looked. I wasn't sure
anymore, and you'd start up again.
Each time you vanished, bloody
and painful this way. Yesterday,
you said you didn't want to keep
doing this. I wondered about the soul,
if that was something you ate up too,
something I didn't build for you.

MISTER SNUFFLEUPAGUS

You wouldn't know it but I'm Mister Snuffleupagus

Big Bird's best friend on a street called Sesame

It took a lot of work to be Mister Snuffleupagus

No one really knows that

I did it for two and a half years

Big Bird told me "Most people don't last that long"

I didn't want to be Mister Snuffleupagus

I did it for Big Bird

I thought he could really use a real friend

I went to the audition and I got the part

Each week there was a new audition and I always made the cut

I don't really know why

Maybe they were impressed I did it all by myself

It usually took a team of two or three to be him

I blinked his eyes and fluttered his eyelashes

I moved all four legs, that tail and trunk

I smiled on cue

I sang and swayed and propped him up

All the lines I had to memorize

All the staying-out-of-the-way I did

There were others who had been Mister Snuffleupagus

But no one played that part as good as me

Maybe you noticed something different about him

When I was Mister Snuffleupagus

I noticed something different about Big Bird

He was happy

The view I had from inside the suit

I watched all the friends who came

And never saw me

I watched all the games you played

I never got to play them with anyone but Big Bird

He had me all to himself

I loved Big Bird

I guess that's the reason I came back each week to audition

Big Bird and I knew each other without our costumes

We had seen the other's face

He let me see his face

He said something about love and he took off his head

I took my head off too, but it was because I knew what I was

Big Bird told me I could be replaced

Anyone could be Mister Snuffleupagus, he said

I argued back

It's not true, I said

Only I could be Mister Snuffleupagus

The same way only he could be Big Bird

That year he turned forty-two

The year he knew the answer to life, the universe, and everything

But he didn't know the question

I was there

I was there when the room filled with the friends he wanted

I was good at having feelings and having fun

But that isn't proof of anything

Feelings

I was the expert at the small joys

The one who asked all the questions

After a while, I got tired of not being seen

I knew what I was

I stopped auditioning

My scenes were there in full colour

My suit was worn and held up by others

It happens to everyone, I guess

Not long after I had been gone

Everyone else moved out of the neighbourhood

Even the grouchy guy in the garbage can

Friends stopped coming over for dinner

Big Bird doesn't know why that is

I do

When I was there

I knew what I was

I was Mister Snuffleupagus

That's why

Big Bird moved out of the neighbourhood too

There were other Mister Snuffleupaguses I am sure

The show, after all, has to go on

But none were like me

Big Bird would never say that

Not to me

It would mean there was something behind all the play

Something real

Just because you have nothing to show for it

It doesn't mean it wasn't real

All the children are still there

Grown up now, of course

They don't know what I made and did for them

And those who have taken my scenes don't know what I broke

They don't know I spit those words in that mouth first

I want to say what I never got to say

That I was there

That it was me

That it was mine

It all belonged to me

I was there when it all happened

At the beginning

You won't find that in his stories or his books

Not even a footnote or appendix

There isn't a record of it

Happiness embarrasses Big Bird

He can't believe in it

To keep his revolution going

He won't ever say it

So I will say it for myself

Because I live in this world too

Notes

1. "Sunrise with Sea Monsters" – see J. M. W. Turner's painting

2. "O" – https://www.theguardian.com/world/2008/dec/03/laos-cluster-bombs-uxo-deaths and the July 2018 *New York Times* coverage of the dam collapse in Laos.

3. "There are no American combat forces in Laos" – Richard Nixon

4. "North" – lines 4 and 5 are taken from the Weather Network

Acknowledgements

These poems have appeared in the following places: "Cluster" in *The Globe and Mail*; "Mother" as "Third Eye" in *This Magazine*; "Minute Maid Poster" as "Poster" in *Taddle Creek* and a booklet by Academy of American Poets; "Sunrise with Sea Monsters" in Paul Vermeersch's sunrisewithseamonsters. blogspot.com; "A Plastic Bear" as "A Blue Plastic Horse" and "We Always Lived With Mice" in *Hart House Review*; "Pregnant" in *Room Magazine*; "Brokerage Report I" and "Brokerage Report II" in *Canada and Beyond*; "A Seahorse" in *Arc Magazine*; "Gayatri" in *The Walrus*, Best Canadian Poetry (2016), and Best of Best Canadian Poetry (2017); "Zevart" published as a broadside by Junction Books; "Brokerage Report V" in *Canadian Notes & Queries*; "My Mother Gave Me" in *Brick*; "Cost" as "Squirrel" in *Lao American Review*; "Twins" in *Maisonneuve*; parts of "O" in *What the Poets Are Doing*; "North" in *The Goose*; "Blowfish" as a limited edition chapbook by Jay and Hazel Millar; "Theory of Writing" in *The Walrus*; and "Mister Snuffleupagus" in *The Puritan*. Thank you to the editors. Thank you to the Ontario Arts Council Works in Progress and Writers' Reserve programs. Thank you to the University of Ottawa and their writer-in-residence program. Thank you to the Guggenheim Museum and Academy of American Poets.

Souvankham Thammavongsa is the author of three poetry books, *Light* (2013), winner of the Trillium Book Award for Poetry; *Found* (2007); and *Small Arguments* (2003), winner of the ReLit Award. Her writing has appeared in *Harper's, Granta, Brick, Best American Nonrequired Reading*, and other places. She has been in residence at Yaddo and has performed her work at the Guggenheim Museum in New York. She was born in the Lao refugee camp in Nong Khai, Thailand, and was raised and educated in Toronto.